You Looked at me too.

I saw you today, sitting alone in a theatre lobby-
and though there were people surrounding,
you still seemed lonely.

And as I walked by, I was too nervous to look
into your eyes,
but I felt a surge of regret upon exiting,
knowing that if you had looked at me too,
your eyes would have shone like star light,
and perhaps I would have had the courage
to say "hi".

I know you looked at me too.

Oh, and you were so beautiful,
I wanted you right then and there;
but doubt is an evil friend,
and while protective at times,
it can destroy so many hidden worlds.

I saw you today, sitting alone in a theatre lobby-
and though you were lonely, I did not say "hi".
And I know, as I walked away...
I know you looked at me too.

A Hindrance Unknown

The snow will melt, the grass turned green, but
when you look, I am unseen.
Beneath this rock, shall I lay, for years to
come, and you decay.
From my mind swept clean, and mouth a-
scream, begging for the light to be seen.
Into the ocean afar, I stay adrift, my body
aglow, like the gleam of a star.
Dipped into space with little unknown, your
eyes watch with care, a button unsown.
From my heart dead and dry, now buried
beneath, to your solemn watching eye, with
clenched, biting teeth.

A Sealant for the Cracks in your Soul

The cracks can be found everywhere.

In the walls,
the ceiling,
and the off white door that leans solemnly
against the wall.

Black as paint,
white as chalk,
it is a contrast that is stark and slightly
unbearable.

Yet there is a peace here,
in these cracks on the wood.

They are the slits that split the "r" found in the
word "broken".

They are the proof that there has been
damage.

But with every crack,
there is a seal.

And that is what he is,
you foolish,
beautiful young girl.

He is your sealant for the cracks in your soul.

A Train Collision of Commotion

Notes about worlds that lie between human
thoughts
are scattered on my floor,
while a tainted hand paints my door.

Lines of black trickle down a white screen
in which only I can see;
Can you hear it, or is that only me?

There is a train collision of commotion
screaming
through my head,
while a brown cat lies sleeping in my bed.

Too many things going on at once in this
dreary state of mind; it's like a pulsing ache,
catapulting through my time.

Tick,tock,Tick,Tick,
the clock is broken, but time keeps moving,
marching forward,
to my life, I'm losing.

White noise in my ears and sandpaper in my
tears;
Will the agony overcome my fears,
or will I start dying,
in this year?

I hope I do soon,
because I want to meet the moon.

So kill me sweetly,
rape me blind;
kiss me gently,
while I stay kind.

Because tonight I want to end my life;
make it slow, and stop my strife.

All I Can See

Rose red, color in my head;
the taste on my tongue, the quake in the sun,
when our lips collide, hearts coincide, and
chaos ensues on the dance floor.
Black lashes, whips and sashes;
the feel of your skin, this thing called "sin",
when my nails bite down, voice creates sound,
and stillness falls around us.
White cheeks, collar and leash;
the grip on your throat, the brush and the
stroke, when I kiss down your back, brain in a
wreck, and the pounding starts again.

All that is you, all that is me; all that is us, that's
all I can see.
And it's driving me mad, I'm going insane; your
spirit's so wild, your lips are so tame.

I want it all, I need much more; hold me tight,
make me sore;
and watch me dance around your soul; I need
your beauty, I need control;
to lead you farther into my mind; I know you'll
love just what you find;

because all that is you, all that is me; all that is
us, that's all I can see.

Amongst the Reeds and Rushes

Amongst the reeds and the rushes you ran,
With plimsoll, pinafore precociousness,
I watched you, amongst the weeds and the
bushes.
Starched skirts enwrapped us, the flowers
would match us
We missed the noontime sun. The evening
drew
Its hand over the day, the dusk would catch us.
In warmth, through my weighty eyes, I awoke.
Calm wine left in the basket had lulled me and
As I watched you play, I imagined how
Each blossom spoke, each stigma gave you
words.
My conversation had passed, my tongue grew
dry
I forget their speech, the songs of the birds.
And as I watched your joy with each bound
renew,
I watched my voice grow old as it called out to
you.

And I, oh Dear, I was Cruel

I want your sins wrapped closely with mine,
under a lavender parasol
discarded amongst the highway trash,
where only we can be sheltered
from the torrents of rain,
pattering gently outside our shadowed fort,
trickling through the pines in the distance,
where muffled howls call our names.
You want me to forget how we once fell,
into an ocean of bed
with legs tangled and
hair, so matted, giggles
echoing around four covered walls,
the only witnesses to our trials
being thickly printed paper
and pocket watches,
ticking our time away.
I need you to remember who we were,
innocents lost to a world
that lashed our backs
and chained you down,
with thoughts plagued by guilt
for something we'd done,
purely by choice-
and I, oh dear, I
was cruel.
And you needed me to understand that
it was not just a game, nor just a
curiosity. No, you needed me to hold you

and whisper delicacies in the form
of tightly wrapped roses,
dipped in caresses, coos, and
the truth that I,
myself, was blind to see.

And yet...
I want your sins wrapped closely with mine,
under a lavender parasol
discarded amongst the highway trash,
where only we can be sheltered
from the torrents of rain,
pattering gently outside our shadowed fort,
trickling through the pines in the distance,
where muffled howls call our names.

Arabesque

I'm not too sure what it means.
But left to my imaginings, I'd say that it stands
for comfort.
The comfort of *home*.
Of joy, the warmth of love.
It is a song, it is a feeling,
It is everything I dream of;

and it is so far beyond my reach.

Oh, how I long for arabesque.
How I wish to find it, here and now.
But alas,
It is still beyond my reach-
For in a world so grotesque,
I cannot hope to find that feeling;

the feeling of arabesque.

Beautiful Fears

Candle whispers in the dead of night,
stone cold crawlers move away from light;

Their scales are spiny,
their lips so grimy;

I hate them yet I love them,
their eyes so tiny;

Piercing mine with putrid lust,
their nails digging with sordid rust;

Keep them close,
but hold them at bay;

Stroke their feathers,
ignore what they say;

Because they will love you,
despite their sneers;

They are your demons,
your beautiful fears.

Blue Birds

In the ever-changing canvas that is your heart
and mind, there is an effervescent echo darting
between time; like the temperamental bass
resounding in your voice, we have many
options that lead to one choice.
When I walked in the room, I found chaos
and scars, giving us a reason to drive out to
mars; to watch the world crumble under piles
of rubble, a place full of trouble that leaves us
befuddled.
Through pain and through struggle, your tears
are so subtle, finding their warmth in emotions
so muddled.
But even in fear, I wiped up your tears, kissed
you hello and led you in tow.
The heat in your touch, even when rough,
sinks further down into an ocean profound.
Placing a hand over terrified eyes, you will not
be subject to their only demise.
Escape from reality and sink into space; we'll
forget all our troubles until they're erased.
In death do we part, because that's where we
start, to trip into thought, till dead do we drop.
And just as I said, we'll watch the Earth set, the
grass turning grey, flying like blue birds,
far, far way.

The Box

This box is big.
This box is small.
It's keyhole stares at me,
darkness enthralled.
I try to unlock it;
I've used every key.
But a rusted keyhole,
won't let me succeed.
It holds many secrets,
so many thoughts,
things I can't decode,
feelings made of dots.
This box is too big,
This box is too small...
But even if I tried,
it won't open at all.

Beautiful, Black Hair

Mow the lawn,
Cut the hair,
Trim the beard,
Sit and stare,
As she drops her dress,
Show those thighs,
Flutter her lashes,
Baked lil' pies.

Smirk the lips,
Tame the dog,
It'll all come soon,
Don't get me wrong;
She's a damn sexy lady,
With hips so lush,
Breasts nice and round,
And that natural blush.

Ride her body,
All night long,
Take her to a movie,
Sing her a song;
Till you take her to bed,
Pop open the wine,
Sip a lil' whisky,
Damn, she's lookin' fine.

And her long hair is bouncing,
She's raking your chest,

Keep up the tempo,
Make this your best;
Because she leaves in the morning,
When you're not aware,
That silent, cruel dame,
The one with beautiful, black hair.

Butterfly Blue

One light in the dark.
Pulsating neon.
Robins egg, single but paired.
Fly,
Fly away.
Brighten his path.
Only one, single yet paired,
May guide him.
Only you,
Butterfly Blue.

Red Wood

The red of the wood.
So fine and clean.
Harsh to the trembling touch,
of a young girl so in love with its beauty.
She tells the men of her story.
Dull gray eyes staring far into the past,
and memories flooding like even tide.
To wash away her happiness.
To remind her.
Of the red of the wood.
So fine and clean.
Harsh to the trembling touch,
of a young girl so in love with its beauty.

Clarity

This is my guiding light-
My reason for existing.
This is that once-in-a-lifetime moment,
Where you have to grab hold of it by the
throat,
Throw it against a wall and watch it melt against
the paint.

This is a time of deep meaning,
Of chilling reality under a midnight sky.
Wearing only the skin on your bones,
You pin it tight under your weight,
Goosebumps racing down your spine;
This is the moment.
And that moment is called
Clarity.

Cherry Rose Stem

Let me whisper your name
Let it course through your veins
As my hands grab your waist
Pulls you in for embrace
Under a bleary night sky
Where the stars hear you sigh
With pleasure and joy
I swear I'm not being coy
When I kiss your sweet lips
And take tiny sips
Of the words that you speak
As I feel you go weak
My hands drinking you in
This must be a sin
It's so devilishly good
As I knew that it would
Be a sumptuous dream
A grand kind of scheme
In which our bodies do meet
From my head to your feet
And twine into one
Under a bright yellow sun
Our breath coincides
My hands caressing your thighs
And you suddenly gasp
Words turn into rasps
When my tongue dips inside
My God, you're in for a ride
And I can't go back now

You might wonder how
I can love you so much
When my heart starts to rush
Spilling up, spilling out
And you start to shout
Nails biting into skin
How does it end?
With passion and grace
No words can replace
That long final scream
To let off some steam
And relax into me
You'll finally see
That you are my only
So you'll never be lonely
My priceless little gem
Set upon a cherry rose stem.

<u>DayByDay</u>

There's something there,
    crawling slowly and steadily into the back on
                        my brain.
I can't place it,
  this grotesque feeling of something going awry
                        in the world.
But little by little,
daybyday,
it grows stronger.

And with each setting of the sun,
    my resolution to continue further onward
    becomes paper thin, until, sometime soon,
            it just might wither away.

Defining You

Upon he be the wrath of the Devils;
Hidden thoughts and emotions,
Shrouded in clouds of purple-black mist.
So many masks;
Some of pain,
Others desire,
Much in Joy,
Shredded in fire.
Years spent behind this door,
Hiding everything.
When did it change for you?
Can you remember?
Or have you already...
Forgotten?

Dee

We're standing in an ocean scene, feet
brushing crystal sand.
Rain sprinkles down in droplets, so I smile and
take your hand.

"Would you like to go back?" I whisper, soft
and clear.

You shake your head and answer, "I'd rather
we stayed here."

Our eyes meet for a moment, and I look away
real fast.
"Why do you do that?" You wonder, and now
I feel like an Ass.

"You make me nervous." I admit, ashamed and
blushing mad.
"Oh, okay." You reply, voice gently soft and
sad.

I turn to look and brush your cheek, frowning
at what I see.
Eyes of worry, smile gone, this saddened girl
named Dee.

I hug you close and gently whisper, "Please
forgive me, dear."

You shake your head and smile in answer, "I'm no one you should fear."

For a moment we stay quiet, peaceful in embrace.
I pull out my camera, snap a picture, smiling at your face.

You're blinking in surprise, eyes wide with confusion and shock.
I dance away when you try to catch me, racing for the dock.

We're laughing when we board, a boat I like to call "Free".
I labeled it after her spirit, this little girl named Dee.

Wet and soaked, we don't care, we motor away from harbor.
She's smiling at me playfully, and resisting is so much harder.

I take her picture, once, twice, another that's just right.
And as we grin, the rain now stops, sun bursting into sight.

One last picture, beautiful as can be, reflecting this boat called "Free".

Suddenly she kisses me, blush blooming on
her face, this lovely girl named Dee.

But then the rain comes back, blocking light
from view.
We rush back to land, docking, running right
on cue.

So the rain falls harder and we start laughing,
ducking under cover.
Your hair is wet and we're both drenched, yet
we giggle like famous lovers.

As we wait for the bus to whisk us away, I ask
you one more question.
"Do you love me, Dee?" And you fall silent, my
body stiff with tension.

You turn and look me dead in the face, eyes
full of steel and wire.
Then you kiss me frisky, hot and heated, lost
forever in fire.

Now as the rain lets up, I open my eyes and
grin at what I see.
Eyes of light, smile of laughter, this beautiful
girl named Dee.

Father God

Stars have fallen upon his shoulders and
scattered about the land,
blazing brilliant rainbows of light that streak
across the night,
rip apart the dark,
tear into sight,
and disappear.

His fingers ghost across the piano keys in the
sky,
playing angelic notes that scatter through air,
cascade down from the stars,
tumble without care,
and repeat.

Clouds are his resting place above the heavens,
shadowing every constellation that drifts by,
skips across galaxies,
pauses from its fly,
and rests.

Drip, Drop, Drip

In private company she walks.
Separate, but not knowing.
They're leading her on, using those coaxing
words of comfort.
A fool is she, the gullible one, her innocence
taking the better of her.
She's guided in silence now, a heavy air
surrounding as they draw closer.
She sees in the distance those same buildings,
the ones she always walked past, on beautiful
Tuesday afternoons.
They were striking against the sky, the weather
still a blur to her mind.
Was it cloudy?
Or cold?
Windy maybe?
Possibly sunny?
Still, she couldn't tell.
It was then that she heard only one pair of
steps.
Alone was she.
But her feet drew her near, guided the body
forward like gravity.
Something was screaming, telling her;
RUN!
STOP!
TURN BACK!
But she is a fool.
Blood drips from her temple.

It slips lazily down her cheek.
Drip from her jaw,
Drop to caress the pavement below.
Drip, Drop, Drip.
Onward she went.
Slip, Slide, Slip.
The buildings coming forward.
Drip, Drop, Drip.
Sweaty hands in pockets; she's here now.
Slip, Slide, Slip.
She sees the crimson.
The stain of red upon her crisp, white shirt.
She turns and sees her beloved.
Standing with a twisted smirk.
The knife now firmly implanted.
Mission accomplished.
Her head meets pavement.
As the blood slowly, but surely,
Drips.Drops.Drips.

Falling For You

I am secretly falling for you.

Steadily, and with so much emotion-

It trickles downward, much like the rain does,
when it's barely misting;
each trembling droplet finding each other to
form something so much bigger, in their quest
to slip lazily across your car's spotted
windshield.

But oh, my dear, there is so much color to it.

Unlike the clear, watery tears that you kissed
from my eyes, this feeling is vibrant and warm,
like summer's soft, pulsing yellow,

But also

Pine Bark Brown, the color of your eyes;

Violently Red, the warmth in my cheeks;

Deep Ocean Black, the whiskers on your chin;

Baby Soft Pink, my lips when you kiss them.

And oh, so many colors, they're impossible to
list!

But somehow you grasp them tightly and place them,
so very gently, deep into my heart-

And it creates a beautiful mix.

I am secretly falling for you, and though the time has been short, I can confess to you the many reasons that you've nestled your soul so closely with mine.

Like how, when we're lying together, you can't seem to keep still-
Your foot always tapping, muscles subconsciously twitching, hands moving over mine.

And how your lips are always near me, whether it be my
Hair,
Cheek,
Neck or shoulder.

Then there's the way that your eyes never stray from me for too long-
You think I don't notice, but sweetie, it's hard to miss.

And God, I'm falling for you daily, but it's something I must keep to myself.

Because if there's one thing I'm scared of at
this very moment,

It's losing you, like I've lost so many before.

So I'll keep falling for you,
But only steadily-
And with colorful, beautiful, overwhelming
emotion.

Frothing

I found myself in a field of flowers
With mind frothing and body shaking,
Stopping short of seizing entirely
And falling prey to grief.

I found myself in a locked closet
And could I see the way my body laid,
Twisted and torn as it was,
I do not think I would have moved to fix it.

I found myself under the bed,
Hiding from the world
Denying existence,
Cutting myself off from all that is joy.

But no matter how many times I found myself,
I only managed to lose myself again.

Fools

It isn't until this night that We realize :: We
Are Fools.

We, the slaves of Immaturity.
We, the idiots of impulsive behaviors.
Us, the rabbits trapped under caged-in holes.
Us, the humans with the "bright" ideas.

Think Outside Of The Box.

Grab your flashlights,
Put on a coat;
We're going to the forest,
With nowhere to go.

Put on your shoes,
Tighten your scarf;
We're rolling in snow for an hour,
And hoping we don't barf.

Leave your ipods,
Abandon your phones;
We're gonna swim in the ocean,
And smash tiny gnomes.

Remember Responsibility.

Don't go to sleep,
Don't go outside;

You've got a paper to write,
Not a fun car ride.

Drink your coffee,
Smoke your grass;
Finish the cleaning,
Don't fall on your ass.

Stress is your buddy,
Make her your wife;
She's really quite nice,
The cutting Bitch-Knife.

Pick A Side.

It's not all that hard.

Would you rather wake,
With a face old and fake,
Eyes worn with wear,
And bruised purple on pear?

Or scream at the sun,
Run for the fun,
Bake an ice-cream cake,
And smile for only your sake?

Either Way...
It isn't until this night that We realize ::
We.

Are.
Fools.

For Freddy

Rest easy now, there's no time to fret;
you have too much to smile for, so never forget
the lullabies and the stories, the rhymes by
Shel Silverstein;
the ruckus and rowdy, to help
blow off some steam.

I do declare that there is no such place as
Where the Sidewalk Ends,
because nothing is permanent,
it all just depends;
on where we go in life, or even in death;
whether we experience strife, or grasp at what's
left.

It feels like you're drowning in a rather large
cup,
but if you reverse the falling down, you'll start
Falling Up;
and it's important you remember,
that you open your eyes and see;
just how much your smile,
makes you a great Giving Tree.

Forks

I watched you tumble down the hill
in a literal sense
and it was the happiest,
most joyous day of your life,
even with grass stains on your white shirt
and sticks in your wild brown hair.

You saw me turn the corner
and a smile lit your face
like the sun had just burst
from a long, hard day
of cloudy skies,
and it was the most beautiful thing
I'd ever seen.

I heard the sound your heart made
when you stared at my back
as I got into the car
and drove far, far away,
and it was the worst day for us both,
and it has yet to get any better,
even after all this time.

And I leaned back against the cold, thick
pole in the park
and looked up at the autumn sky
as the sun set over the buildings
and the city lights came on,
one by one,

until they were the only light
seen for blocks in either direction,
leaving me in the dark
next to the swings I loved so much.

Nothing can be said;
can only be thought,
by a mind lost in the trees,
split by too many forks,
and not enough posts
to guide it back home.

From Fantasy, to Reality

There is a little girl,
stuck alone in her little world.

It's a wonderful place, really.

So many beautiful creatures,
Vast, open space,
Plentiful sun and warmth,
And millions of kind things.

And as she daydreams,
this little girl,
she hears a tiny tap upon her door.

Could it be,
she wonders,
My beloved friend the Griffin?

So,
with a smile she pranced,
down the stairs,
and without a care,
opened her door,
to let him in.

Four months have passed.

Her mother sits by the casket,
father covering his face with his hands.

And they listen,
listen as the preacher talks,
talks of their little girl,
who had the biggest imagination,
and could not tell,

From fantasy,
To reality.

Further Beyond

When it crashes down, it crashes in waves.

Her ears are red, her heart inflamed.

She sits alone, in the dark she stares, at the
ticking clock, that needs repairs.

It's incessant,
It's constant,
It won't go away;

It's shouting,
It's screaming,
Time for another day!

But she doesn't get up,
In bed she stays,
while the sun still rises,
and her heart decays.

She's never quite known such distasteful
despair;
She now knows how he felt, abandoned
without care.

She feels like she's shrinking, under torrents of
rain, shriveled and unwanted, tortured with
pain.

And now the moon rises,
And she'll sit and she'll wait;
Alone in her silence,
Alone with her fate.

Because nothing else matters,
and without her she's gone,
into cursed oblivion,
and further beyond.

Half-Wilted, Half-Stable

You came to me in the night, half-wilted, half-
stable,
hand reaching through darkness in search of
mine.
You wished for me to take it, as if in some sort
of fable,
and I merely sat stoic, listening as the clocks
ticked out the time.
But instead of taking offense, you pulled up a
chair,
sat right next to me,
and rested that hand over mine.
I pulled away once or twice, scared of the
warmth,
how it thawed out the shell I'd crafted over the
clocks' tolls and chimes-
until, just barely, I felt the depth of your touch,
soft and so simple, yet rough and still fickle;
the touch of an angel, one that I already loved
so much.
Then it was gone, like a flash in the dark-
leaving behind a rather loud silence;
air bitter and stark.
I waited too long, that much I know-
so here I sit, quiet and pitiful,
chilled by winters' oncoming snow.
And this time I'll work harder, to thicken my
shell-
no one shall touch me again,

I'd sooner go to Hell.
And you left me in the night, not wilted, only
stable-
hand reaching out to someone else, forgetting
about mine.
They took it, they claimed it, and handed you
a fable;
while I sat wilted, not stable, the clocks ticking
away the time.

Just Like Human

Cherish these moments,
In which we live such peaceful lives;
With quiet contradiction and silent conviction.

Though we hate with passion
And love with loathing,
We remain one;
Equal.

Do not praise me;
Do not bow;
Do not thank me.

For just like you,
I stand in the light of day,
With shadows exposed and rotting.

Intimacy

To be physically intimate with someone is to
reach into the bottomless depths of the ocean,
and pull out a rare,
green
rose.

It will glimmer and shine like her eyes when
she looks at me,
but then it will prick and,
in time,
draw blood.

But to feel that sting and see the crimson is to
shiver with anticipation,
knowing that,
soon,
she'll kiss me.

Into the Sky Again

She thought about her for the first time in
years and
   In the process, she'd somehow slipped out of
                                 her skin-
and fallen into the sky again.

   Where the ocean met the Universe, that's
           where she fell,
stiff skin lathered in dark matter, it slithered up
her arms and caressed her gently between the
        thighs;
    a feeling unknown to anyone else.

   She thought about her for the first time in
              years and
Because of this, she's floating gently between
the surfaces of a dark, warm ocean
      and a beautiful, silver-stained sky.

She lives in a body wracked with the weight of
  disease; her heart is twisted and worn, mind
    sluggish with despair-
but none of that matters here, when thinking
    about her, because
She can feel the stars slip gracefully across her
  torso and make their way into her soul.

So when she thought about her for the first
time in years,

she turned her head to rest against the clouds,
as she fell out of her skin and back, way back
into the sky again.

Kindly, Kind of, Confused

Your eyes hold no bearing to the future.
Big and bright as they are,
Kindly confused and chastise withheld,
You hold me here in the bonding grasp that is
your calming presence.
Your voice and laugh are the air I breathe,
A second nature to me,
If you will.
Don't you realize how far we've come?
From mere acquaintance,
To buddy and friend,
Then practically a sister,
And now a love like fire.
You don't notice,
I'm sure.
But if so,
Your eyes reveal nothing to be seen.
Some days I hope,
Some nights I pray,
Wondering;
Will you reject me?
The thought that stays awake within gnaws
frantically;
Always on the edge of my conscious,
Asking and taunting;
When will your kindly confusing eyes finally
see...
And finally refuse?

Let it all Burn

Countless thoughts of destroying worlds.
Tyranny has never looked so beautiful through
these eyes.
Comprehension of wanting to tear down the
people of the land,
it suddenly becomes so clear.
To see their fear, and to taste their blood;
the urge grows stronger each and every second.
Let's watch them burn,
and together,
only we will rule.
It is my greatest wish that we do.

<u>Losing</u>

A thousand millennia and still I am awake.

Tortured and useless, dragged across concrete,
my body remains a lone vessel waiting
departure,
recapture,
or a sick combination of the two.

Warped is my stomach,
bleeding is my brain;
I'm made to leave,
and forced to go,
but my will and my soul remains.

Here in the lights,
there in the streets,
under the dirt,
blanketed within music.

Further onward and tear myself to shreds,
I will.
Cast me into flame and watch me burn,
but I am the fire and the fire is me,
so I laugh it away and fight once more.

Tyranny triumphs in my mind,
where I am God and no one controls me
better than,
well,

me.

So I raise my eyebrows in obstinate opposition,
daring myself to come a little closer,
dancing with the she-devil that is at war
within her own lair.

We scrap for days and then come the blades;
only one death is really guaranteed.

But two of the same,
fighting one war?

Annihilation has never been so beautiful.

I'll slice myself through and through,
till the blood of pain drains away,
and revel and bask in the glorified light of a
whole new life.

But even then,
that is just me again,
dealing myself a deck I never wished for.

Perhaps, in this way,
the game can finally end.

Because,
after all,
I am the only one losing.

Lost-Love Collector

The stars are weeping tears of fire,
and upon the Earth they will fall.
My mind is full of tracks of tires,
until she makes her final call.
~

Confusion sweeps me,
makes me sick,
and I unravel,
watch her tick.
~

She has this power,
don't get me wrong;

Her love is like music,
a beautiful song.

Wrapping me close,
holding me tight;

Stuck on my toes,
nothing to fight.
~

Because he is forgotten,
a memory swept away,
and though I am rotten,
I don't care, I won't sway.

I love her so dearly,
her heart my only treasure,

for I am but merely,
her lost-love collector.

Love in a Rhyme

Powder blankets the land in glistening white,
and my love grows here in the dead of night.

It's quiet and peaceful,
like when we lie in my bed;
I wish to kiss you,
and listen to what you've said.

We can roll in the grass,
get real cold and wet;
Snuggle for hours,
until the sun sets.

And then our night will begin,
cold and quite thin;
Until I break that shy ice,
and sprinkle you with spice.

So as the snow falls and thickens in time,
I'll tell you I love you with this simple rhyme.

Points

I'm writing a poem about nothing in particular.
It's more like a collection of thoughts, really.
Something about sacrilegious acts,
Stale cookies in plastic bags,
Two cats fighting it out,
Fake love of some sort,
Uncommitted sexual encounters,
Perfect lips tainted with lies,
Glowing neon remotes,
Absurd sights of horses nuzzling cows,
Purple clothing,
Wooden fans, cheese nips, meatballs on fire,
white doors, robot boys, condoms...
...what was my point again?

Maybe Another Day

Write to me your feelings.

Maybe a simple song would do.

Perhaps you wish to scold me;
You were always good at that, too.

I keep your words on paper,
because they are very dear to me.

But take it all back,
and you'll never see;
these tears that will fall,
the happiness, it'll flee.

And you know,
that's okay.

I'll live,
I'll smile,
Maybe Another Day.

But for now I will frown,
and look the other way,
until I can smile,

on that far-off,
distant day.

Memories in the Park

Do you remember those nights, oh
loved ones?
Glorious days set into dark, with twinkle stars
to light the land we played on.

In that park, so distant and far in the
haze of my memories?
When the chills sparkled through my veins,
but the warmth of my blankets kept me there.

And those swings, so many songs sang
upon their seats?
As the moon would cast my body into
silhouette, and my words would rise to the sky.

Don't you remember, the days we played tag?
We ran till our lungs were sore and our feet
cried out, but we still laughed.

And your smiles were never-ending, like the
blue above our heads?
The jokes ran continuously, and we never
wanted to stop.

Until the moon rose to it's peak, and silence
was only to speak?
Till our words came back, but with a calming
ring.

Did you forget, young ones?
Days and nights mixed into one, the setting of
the moon and the sun.

For hours on end, when the kids were
there and the time we'd spend?
Cuddled up close, forgetting our clothes.

Cell phones would ring, and I'd stop to
sing?
Just one last time, before I went home, and
forgot how to rhyme.

Do you remember, oh loved ones?

Black Tar

The wind stood chillingly still in the vast
recesses of my cavernous mind,
where oceans crash in heaving torrents upon
the shores of my thoughts,
bearing with them a current that weighs down
in a pond of black tar.

The muscles within my arms contract fiercely
against this devilish force,
flexing and stretching until I can feel each
tendon tearing with strain.
But no matter how much I might wish to swim,
I am stuck in the waste of eighteen lost years.

Could I see you now,
I'd be looking up once again,
toward a beacon of light that does not exist.

I am swamped under unbearable words.
Thoughts that once sunk down into my depth
are unearthed in this hour.

And I stare at them with vulgar.

My hand, covered in sweat so slimy and putrid,
twitches upward and outward.
And yet it does not move.

Heavens' gates are closed tonight,

as they are many a night,
standing tall and leonine,
away from my reach.

This is the land where Hell speaks its name
like the toll of a medieval bell.

Our Time

The taste of tabs is strong on my tongue, and
the feel of his skin reminds me of rum;
strong, yet soothing, with a bit of a burn --
a feeling that leaves me wanting to learn --
more about you, more about us;
How far can we go, without causing a fuss?

The tingle of 5 o'clock shadow lingers on my
lips;
I want to grip you by the collar and press into
your kiss.

You're sexy as Hell, so rugged and tall --
Don't stop touching me, babe,
while I fall and I fall --
over your body, draped in hot sweat;
you keep me alive, you make me so wet.

So keep the drugs coming, let's block out our
minds --
Because, after all, this is our time.

Mexico

I remember how,
When we first met,
You were the one to smile first,
And introduce yourself,
When you sat next to me in that dark room,
Aboard a cruise line set for Mexico.

I remember being immediately drawn to you,
Despite your demeanor, and wanting to know
you more,
After only one short conversation,
In which you made me laugh, and
complimented me.

The details are fuzzy on how exactly we
continued from there,
But I recall brief flashes of
Running around on deck,
Meeting new friends,
Playing assorted games,
Swimming in the salt-laced pools,
The way you pressed yourself firmly against
me,
Unabashed, unafraid, of the glaring sun
And prying eyes.

But most of all, I remember the way your dark
eyes gleamed when they looked down at me,
Atop that magnificent vessel,

Stars surrounding,
Love songs playing,
Closing in to make your move.

You teased me a little, asking what I wanted,
Even when you knew the answer;
And I was just too shy to say it.

So you said it for me by
Taking that last step,
Surrounding my body entirely
With your presence,
Grabbing hold of my face
And kissing me like I'd never been kissed
before.

Somehow I knew that night would be the
beginning,
And also the end,
Of that innocent little girl my father called
"princess".

They say it's never possible to hit rock bottom
Unless you've soared at the very peak of bliss.

What a fucking understatement.

Four years
Since that beautiful week,
In which I met you, kissed you,
Fell for you,

And listened as you told me you had someone
back home.

Four years
Since then,
And I straddled your soul,
Followed you through every alley,
Felt your touch behind closed doors,
Took on the label "Mistress",
And still hopelessly vowed to make you mine,
One day.

Four long years, and yes,
The time did come,
When you introduced yourself to my family,
Told me you loved me,
Asked me to be "your girl",
And finally claimed my most valued
possession-
One you knew my father would have killed to
protect.

Four years, five months, and three days.
Bliss, oh, bliss.
I once knew what that felt like.
Bliss, to me, was
Stroking your hair,
Sitting in your lap,
Kissing your cheek,
Telling you good night,
Hearing you say, "I love you".

Bliss was found in your arms.

Four years, five months, three days, and
fourteen hours.
Despair. Yeah, fucking despair.
I know what that feels like.
Despair, to me, was
Sitting on a fucking curb,
Across from a friends' house,
Waiting patiently for you to get past the strain
in your voice,
Already knowing what was coming,
And listening to you as you confessed
How you'd slept with someone else.
Listening to my pulse shatter,
Listening as you cut me off,
Listening as you stood from the cement,
Walked to your fucking car,
And drove the fuck away.

Despair is stumbling to the park,
Falling to the ground,
Curling into a ball,
And sobbing into the dirt.

Despair is being forced to call a friend,
For fear I might do something reckless,
Because there really wasn't a point.

When you left,

You took my heart
And my soul
With you.

Almost six years later,
And I'm just as empty as I was
When it was exactly
Four years, five months, three days, and
fourteen hours
Since I'd fucking met you
During that horrible fucking trip
On a fucking Cruise line
To fucking Mexico.

Moonshine

There are shadows on the wall
in an abandoned shopping mall;
In the eyes of someone aged,
this might look a little staged,
but no one could have known
what this little girl had sewn.

She wandered down a hall that,
in her eyes, looked a bit like a ball;
the darkness was dancing,
the shattered windows glancing,
as she stepped through a door,
that led to a lonely old store.

Dolls lined the shelves,
and above her, hung tiny wooden elves,
all puppets of course,
their strings out of sorts.

She thought of their misfortune,
and how she yearned to reach out and touch
them,
but they shook their bald, dust-covered heads,
and looked back toward the door,
where there lay a pile of threads.

The little girl approached the mound without
any fear,

and the dolls didn't see when she'd shed a lone tear,
as she gathered their hair into her skinny little arms, ran out the door,
and out to the lobby with a dark, open floor.

Setting the pile upon a tiny dry fountain,
she looked to the ceiling that stood tall as a mountain,
where the stars shone through glass and created a spot light,
to set the stage for an innocent child still awake after midnight.

She reached out a vulnerable, shaky hand and opened her eyes wide,
watching the night sky, as it moved and it shifted like a late-evening tide.

Then with a pull of her pinky and a flick of her wrist,
a star came tumbling down in a shower of mist,
engulfing the hair and the mall in one swallow,
the girl disappearing in the event that would follow.

So what happened to the girl and the toys in the store?
Well, the girl is a mystery and the rest is a bore.

The mall was reopened and the toys have a home,
with hair on their heads and someplace to roam.

But right next door, under the light of the moon,
sits   a very old building once used as a saloon.
And if you listen very hard, when the wind blows just right,
you can hear the pitter-patter of feet,
hidden just out of sight.

People of Perfection

Beautiful people with beautiful faces; so many
people in so many places.
Beautiful cheeks to compliment lovely lips;
gorgeous eyes and fingertips.

Narrow nose and clear complexion; clean-cut
hair, dressed to perfection.
People adored and loved- if only! Maybe
they'd smile if they weren't so lonely.

Because beauty brings arrogance and no need
for acceptance;
only greed and hatred, frivolity and
expectance...

...beautiful people with beautiful faces; so
many people in so many places.
But gorgeous eyes see only their reflection;
eyes full of loneliness, these People of
Perfection.

Pick a Card, Any Card

Blue on black,which stands out?
Red or green,is one more vivid?

Well, blue is the sky and black is the cave.
Red is the blood and green is the grass.

Do you lie in the light, or sit in the dark?
Are you drawn to hurt, or bask in peace?

The questions revolve and spin around in
mind and mind.

The wondering, the choosing, the findings and
regrettings.

Let's pick another.

White, perhaps.
Is it scary or bright?
Dull, maybe?
Possibly...evil?

Choose your definition.

Pick a card, any card.

Don't look at it!

Now put it back.

And ask me: "Which one did I choose?"

Hell if I know.

RavenClaw

Tough and bitter ravenclaw,
you cut us deep with skin so raw;
Chew through bone and leave us blind,
your words are sordid and unkind;
My teeth are bleeding with sour despair,
your heart is grieving under your shallow lair;
I hate your words filled with callous,
words so dark they murder with malice;
Leave me be, oh cursed dreams;
you tear me apart by the seams.

Spread your wings and flee in disgrace,
My mind is not your resting place;
For when your flight reaches its peak,
I'll cast my spell and leave you weak;
You'll drop so fast, you'll crow in terror,
And I'll laugh so hard, you'd think it rarer;
to see a blush of comical dismay,
a heart all jumbled in disarray.

This is where you leave me,
oh tough and bitter ravenclaw;
no more will you cut me deep,
no more with skin so raw.

Realism

I tried to battle the wind tonight.
Without any help, my efforts were wasted,
and I was plucked from the ground,
tossed into the sea,
where I sunk to the bottom,
lying in wait;
for what, I do not know;
for whom, I will never know;
but one thing is certain-
I am already dead,
because I cannot breathe down here.

Revolution

Today feels like a Revolution, in which my
mind will tell me what I will do.

These chains that bound me, so unmerciful
and ugly, call me an idiotic fool.

I stare at them, these rustic links, and curse
their blackened face.

No longer am *I* a victim to them or merely a
mouse to chase.

It's on my fingers in which they lay;

and Tomorrow,

Yesterday,

Today,

I have only a few words that I need not say...

So the chains fall down and shatter at my feet;

Their story of an act I refuse to repeat;

Because while I touch that skin and soothe the lust,

I'll remember these chains and their horrible rust.

Those lips will be kissed, but that heart won't be touched;

The heat will get hotter and yet my love will be hushed.

With my hands in the air and my wrists oh, so bare,

I'll cry out my conclusion and show you what I mean;

For today is my calling,

My *Final* Revolution.

Rosemary Spearmint

Yesterday, the thought of death was such a
sweet temptation.
Rosemary spearmint, the scent of peace and
warmth.
Like the dawn beckons children from bed, so
did this aroma lure me forward.
And it was so lovely, so perfect, providing a
trail straight to the cliff's edge.

Feet brushing concrete, eyes looking over; the
bottom is so far below.
Rosemary spearmint, so close, yet so far.
Everyone there, they laughed so joyously, and
sang aloud.
A chorus of off-key voices, ringing out across
silenced lands.

Rosemary spearmint, filling the air, choking in
my lungs.
Peacefully drowning in deaths' wake, as the
music went on.
And I'd never felt so beautiful,
Never felt so free,
Than when I closed my eyes,
Spread my arms, and...
...stood there.

Felt the wind, tasted the sky, and listened as
the world went on.

Knowing that, even in death, nothing would
change.
And so it went on, that night of folly and
merry-making,
While I stared out at the cliff, and very quietly
ignored that scent;
The scent of peace, the provider of warmth;
Rosemary and spearmint.

Sun-Kissed Bungalows

Through your eyes, I've discovered a world
that is beautiful and ever-changing-
Looking within, I can hear the ceaseless
pounding of young hearts flourishing within
grass-stained hills,
a throbbing quartet of innocent lullabies,
and an unending ocean painting a child-like
summer,
where people swim through sun-kissed
bungalows,
and the rain falls upwards toward a sky of
golden-hued waterfalls.
It is through your eyes that I have found peace,
and it is in those eyes I will forever gaze.

Scars

Soft sighs and soft cries resounding through a
bed of lies;
My whispers echo in a dark room and slip past
your uncaring eyes.

You see right through me, as if I am only a
shadow;
Your touch is unmoving, stone cold and so
shallow.

I can't feel the passion, I am devoid of the
heat;
You don't live for me,
I am nothing but meat --

Lying in wait, for you to devour,
when you're feeling feisty,
bored, or too sour.

Why am I like this,
oh foolish me?

I allow you to touch me,
while you are not free.

It's stupid and childish,
this immature game;
I'm merely a girl,
too young and untamed.

I am a soul that's tortured and beaten;
Withered and broken, my heart has been
eaten;
So please leave me be, if your intentions are
wrong --
I don't need this again, my scars are too raw.

Sleeping Like a Kitten

the warmth envelopes my skin and the heat
makes me grin,
because sleep is setting in and I'm cutting this
day thin.

  woke up real sick by the feel of a tough lick,
to the sound of a loud tick and the sweat
running thick.

  got up with a gruff and acted real tough,
though my day got too rough when I couldn't
even huff.

  so I went to the nurse with a frown and a
curse,
wanted to lie in a hearse as she dug through
her purse.

  took a long while but she found my old file,
after I paced a long mile across that white tile.

  then I called up my ma with my voice nice
and raw,
explained my big fall and waited to be clawed.

  she arrived in a flash with her car and her
sash,
so I expected the lash and wished I could dash.

but she smiled with care and hugged me right there,
took me back to my lair and left with no flare.

and now I'm quite smitten with my cats and my linen,
this poem nearly written as I sleep like a kitten.

Slowly Speeding Into the Sea of Mad

Roaming around grassy green prairies in a lazy
summer haze,
my mind rolls about in a warm blanket of
forgetfulness and fretful, foolish denial.

The humidity of the ocean-side beach front
holds my sanity steady in a lukewarm layer of
salty rain,
while the flashing lights of the neon city rock
me to sleep in comforting embrace.

Up and down, the melody goes,
a quartet of rhythm and soft-sounding bass,
harmoniously in sync with the beat of my heart
and the lull of my brain.

This cigarette smoke has glazed my site into
blinded oblivion,
as I slowly speed my way down the stretch of
graveled dirt roads.

Shaking and trembling, I can feel my frame
falling apart.

I've sold myself short and on my knees I now
stand,

while the beat plays so loud and so soothing in
my ears.

In a small sense,
I've lost myself in the Sea of Mad.

But in a bigger sense,
I have plunged deep into black and muddied
waters,
hoping for once that I might never resurface
again.

Starlight Sleeping

Under a cavernous night sky, we feel small and
insignificant -- but not I.

I slept with the stars and I felt their warmth.

They encompassed me, and welcomed me
home, to the universe, and to the heavens.

When I felt their touch, I could not describe it;
my words became knotted in my throat.

If I had to, though, I would say that they are

silky, but creamy;
or brittle, but strong.

They smelt like salt and sweet,
caramel and chocolate,
butterscotch or chocolate-covered raisins.

I wanted to taste them, to see if they were as
sweet as I wanted them to be.

But when I pressed my lips to their mighty
embrace,
I was seared with a burn so hot,
it felt at first like white ice.

They tasted of luminescence and spice.

I woke the next morning with tingling lips and
blinded eyes;
I knew, when I reached my hand to the ceiling,
that the stars had said good night.

I will see them again,
in a Once Upon a Time,
when I am lying in bed,
my mind deep within the depths
of a starlight sleeper.

White

I've got paper in my arms,
Paper on the air,
Paper in my qualms,
Paper on his hair.

It's thick,
It's blank,
It covers everything;
white, White, *WHITE!*
It makes me want to *SCREAM*!

I hate this, **I HATE THIS!**
Silence all around,
I hate this, *I HATE THIS!*
Loneliness profound.

Grit the teeth,
Bear the pain,
Alone I seethe,
Nothing's the same.

Apart we stand,
I can't get back;
Eyes in sand,
Heart made black.

I'm covered in paper,
It covers everything;
white, White, *WHITE!*

It makes me want to *SCREAM!*

but...

alas.

i grit my teeth.

i bear the pain.

alone I seethe.

Nothing's The Same.

Taking Tolls

Ladies and gentlemen, please take your seat!

The show is starting,

right under your feet!

Peer way down,

to the floor below,

and watch the beauty,

as it unfolds.

The music starts with an upbeat tune,

something calming,

something to soothe.

Relax your back against your chair,

but don't be alarmed;

it's attached to thin air!

Now open your eyes,

keep them real wide;

notice the two girls,

as they duck and hide.

Their blushing faces give much away,

the child's game they love to play;

when daylight comes to smile and shine,

I will chase her down and make her mine.

Because the dinosaur roars,

the rocket blasts,

the ships now sail,

and raise their masts.

The girl will hide,

and seek I will,
till we fall,
and take our spill;
on soft grass,
roll and roll,
stop and breathe,
it takes its toll...

Sudden engulfment,
into flame,
her wings spread wide,
her eyes untame!

And I have claws,
a beak and fur,
wings of silver,
eyes to lure!

She is Phoenix,
I am Griffin,
majestic and brilliant,
gentle as kittens.

She will fly, but I will run,
on the clouds, over the sun;
till dawn breaks and I awake,
in her arms and by the lake;
where colors splatter, under my feet,

love at midnight, when we meet;
my rainbow's huge, full of color,
but without my phoenix, I'm pulled under...

Where the girl will hide,
and seek I will,
till we fall,
and take our spill;
on soft grass,
roll and roll,
stop and breathe,
it takes its toll...

The Basics of Appearance

I'd rather not hide these circles under my eyes
because I've created a world behind them in
which I learned to deal
with all the shit this world has to offer.

I'd rather not paint over these scars or highlight
this face
because I've found that sticking to the basics of
appearance
is, at best, the rawest form of holding onto
humanity.

And I'd rather not rid myself of these flaws,
nor mask the wrinkles that are sure to come,
because there's no point in hiding anything,
and with time comes wisdom, thus comes age,
and that's never something that should be
hidden.

No, no, my friends,
I will not hide these circles under my eyes-
I will not paint over these scars,
highlight this face.
I will not
rid myself of these flaws,
nor mask the wrinkles that are sure to come.

Because I have found that sticking to the basics
of appearance

is, at best, the rawest form of holding onto
humanity.

The Girl That Should Rot

Glass upon my wall,
why do you look so tall?
You're showing me things I'd rather not see;
a person so evil, a girl that's not me.

She's the same as before,
blonde hair and all;
but different somehow,
like she's ready to brawl.

How did this happen?
What can it mean?
Have I changed after all,
Have I finally seen?

Who I really am,
what I've already done?
I'm ashamed of myself,
I just want to run.

Away from myself,
away from my friends;
away from the sex,
away from the sins.

For what I have done,
I feel only disgust.
I lie on the floor,
teeth ground into dust.

My body feels dirty,
my soul in dismay;
I'll lie here forever,
until I decay.

I tire of these foolish actions.
I tire of the stupidity, of the terrible attractions.

I am not "I" when I leave my home here.
I am a monster of lust, a whore to be feared.

So return to the city?
Certainly not.

I'm running away,
from the me that is dirty,
from the girl that should rot.

The Last You'll See of Me

Control your thoughts, sweetie.
They might not bring you fortune.
But sometimes, they certainly change the
world.

Your mind is a canvas of beautified texture.
I want to paint it in color, but then leave it
blank.
Contradictions are your pal; I can see it in
those eyes.

The dripping of your faucet reassures me.
It tells me you still haven't changed your way of
thinking.
And for some reason, I'm happy, because that
means you won't be coming back.

Angelic in your style and graceful in your
touch, you mesmerize me, girl.
Your style tells a story of sophistication, with
just of a touch of lazy ease.
I want to take a stroll through your closet and
memorize each stitch of cloth.
Most of all, I want to see those discarded
dressed, the ones you wore when you were
little.

Give me another song that will set my thoughts
afloat, until they drift right back into fog.

Write another poem with my name printed in
every pen stroke.
Selfish and Greedy have no boundaries when
it comes to you, doll.
Only your man keeps me where I lay.

It seems my time is shortening, and I will be
leaving this place soon.
Listen to that song just one more time.
You'll remember why I dedicated it to you
alone.
Because to the sunset I will journey, and with
my back turned to this place, that just might be
the last you'll see of me.

The Soldiers of the Bling, the Mute, and the Deaf

They say that sunsets are beautiful.
Everlasting, they drift out of sight, only to
reappear once more in a timeless cycle.

But what they don't tell you is how sad they
are.
I was driving home from a friends house today
when I saw such a sunset.

It glowed red like the luminescent torch of a
soldier entering war.
But as it made its slow descent, the flame
began to deteriorate.

I thought,
"This soldier has died."

As U2 played softly in the background of my
forethoughts, I revisited the conversation I had
just had with my friend.
His words were said in earnest and I could tell
by the way his dark eyes held such fitful
passion that, in truth, he was right.

When this encounter faded away, my own eyes
took in the sight of soft pink and darkened
blue.
The sky had tilted backwards again, bringing
forth this night in which will always be
remembered.

I was still driving, my body going through all
the familiar notions, and yet I was floating in a
separate dimension.
In this place, this unfamiliar scene, I am
hearing as a blind man hears all the truth of the
world and feeling the touch of a mute man's
screams.

I thought,
"This soldier is in Hell."

But while being assaulted with black-faced
reality, the child within was whimpering to
make it stop.
I only stood there and stroked her soft blonde
hair, calmed her with my voice and reasoned,
'this hill will soon fall flat.'

Her tears pained me greatly; she didn't want to believe what her heart was telling her.
My current state of maturity leveled with the child a calm and assuring eye, just like my father would do.

The mute man and the blind man stood across from me, watching the sky darken in the outer world, and I wondered why they bothered.
The blind man spoke of how he could feel the pressure of the sun lifting off his trodden shoulders, while the mute man simply smiled and nodded in agreement.

I thought,
"These soldiers are brave."

Night has settled and my car is parked in its usual post.
I haven't a clue of what's going on outside; the smell of old cigarettes and my love's perfume perform a dance around my senses as I stare, stunned and remote, out my windshield.

I'm taken back to a time in which I was running; running so far and so fast from eyes as big as cats and that shone like moonshine.

They engulfed my soul in their wake, holding
me paralyzed and unmoving on the steps of
her old apartment, where memories flood into
the surrounding area and sweep me back, far
back, back to my two-story home, where we
once laid.

My room, overlooking a lamp post and small
tree, was dark and quiet as we whispered
excitedly and nervously to each other.
Our sweat was in the air and we complained
about the heat; so we shed our clothes with
giddy giggles and flipped on the fan so we
could lie on the sheets in comfort.

Intensity and passion could not describe the
contact of our skin; hot on cold, water on wine,
black and white mixed together into one big
heap of beauty and star-struck kisses.
We touched and kissed like we'd never done
such things before; it was all new to her and
even new to me, because I had never felt such
a beating in my chest as our every contact sent
rockets cascading down my body in tremors
and shakes that no bomb could match. These
shivers felt **damn** good.

I thought,

106

"Oh. This is love."

Skyrocketed back to reality, my spirit
plummets back into my body, where it sits
curled and dormant in a tub full of lukewarm
and soapy water.
I begin to notice that the blind soldier has
taken over; I can't see, though I don't know
why. He tells me it's because I'm crying.

The mute man seems to have vanished for
now and I'm grateful for that; for him to see
me naked would give me the chills.
Blind soldier seems to find this amusing; he
says to me, 'Aye, lassie, that one's a bit off but
he manages okay.'

He keeps on speaking, but his words are
garbled and he looks to be out of breath at the
moment.
I don't understand his words or even if they're
in the right order, but I guess that's just the
deaf man coming knocking at my eardrums.

Thought returns in a dizzying fashion as I
recall the time in which my angel first kissed
me. At least, I think she's my angel.

It wasn't much to talk of, this wee kiss, but it
certainly did leave its mark. Like a nano bot
planted straight into my muddled mind, it sat
there for future reference like the little bastard
it is.

I thought,
"This certainly is odd."

Yet I went along with it like a foolish duck
dozing off in the backyard pool of a hunter's
home.
Do I regret? Surely not; I enjoyed that first
night, shaken up as I was at the time. I was
betraying my best friend, but hot damn, she
was a tigress-in-action.

I'd never felt such an experienced touch; it
tingled like rows of sparklers brushing my skin,
the fire numb to me at the time, but sure to
come around the bend when she vanished.
And just like that, our night of beastly love
ended. She went home, leaving me at the door,
those sparkler wounds rearing up and making
me burn for more.

I wanted it; I wanted her;

I needed it and I needed her.

I thought,
"You're a God damned fool."

And it went on like that. On and off, flick and
switch, back and forth until our dances became
weary and half-hearted and now we stand, here
on creaking floors, squaring off with unsure
expressions and mouths set to Stubborn.

The world slaps me in the face when I take in
the dust on my shelves; no wonder I can hardly
breathe, aside from the excess smoking.
In an attempt to run from these last thoughts, I
grip my cleaning supplies firmly in hand while
the blind soldier and mute soldier duck for
cover; they positively hate cleaning.

I work my way through hours upon hours until
my room can no longer complain of dirt. But
what am I to do? I've dusted and swept and
cleaned to my heart's content; my thoughts are
running wild and I'm pacing once more!

I thought,

"This soldier has met the General."

The truth is disgusting.
It stares me square in the face as I lie on my
bed.
I think of her and I and what has become of
us; apart and alone, one drunken and
miserable, the other off in her world of art and
friends.

I cling to another like a madman gone even
more insane; I can't bear separation again; it's
my worst fear! Clamping on as tight as possible,
fearful of my memories, using her as a way to
forget about my suffering.
But it's happening again and I cry out, howling
in anguish, the pain searing through me as if I
have just been branded like the cow I know I
am.

I think,
"This soldier is moving onward."

110

The Soldiers of the Blind, the Mute, and the Deaf (Pt. 2)

There was a moment. I felt it, and I knew it was there, but had I not seen it, I wouldn't know. Sitting atop a car with a dented roof; hands aglow but unmoving; it's as if I can no longer see the joy behind these dark, lonely nights.

I thought,
The blind one has returned.

Soldiers, all three, standing in a row behind me. One without sight, one without a voice, the other devoid of sound. They are me, and I am them. If I die, so do they.

What is it that makes them appear?

Ghostly thoughts of past events and even the present, tangling into one. I've been lying in bed, a motionless carving, thinking of the girl that ripped out my soul. Where is she now? Does she think of me at all?
I can only wonder these things, for I am stricken with silence.

I thought,
To be mute is an agonizing thing.

When sitting with him, the boy that I adore as only a sister could, he spoke of his loved one, and how his heart had been set free. I pictured the two of them, together and in love, and I thought about the irony; how they reminded me of our own fairy tale couple, of those long ago nights spent writing up an imaginary world where we could both be happy in each others' arms.

But when reality set in, and my words were spoken, they fell upon ears that would not listen.

I thought,
To be deaf is to be safe.

And so they stand, these worn-out soldiers,
shoulder-to-shoulder,
one listening, one watching, the
other screaming...

...for a solution to this madness.
For an end to the war.
And for a beginning to something new.

Through the Eyes of a Child

Is there a moment in time when I did not
understand, did not
see the beauty of all that was around me?

At a younger time and a different place, I
looked through
the eyes of a baffled and awed child,
wondering
what could possibly make the trees so green
and the waters so blue.

Eyes like that are hard to come by nowadays.

In memory, I do recall dramatizing things a bit;
like the size of my home, which I saw as
colossal and
brilliant as any billion dollar house.

Or the back yard, how its trees and grass were
as tall as mountains or dense as a forest;
the porch swing, possibly the most magical and
wondrous contraption ever invented;
my closet, the cave in which all my worst
nightmares resided;
even my father, who was a kind and gentle
giant, seen as my guardian angel in all respects.

But if I were to visit there now, I would find
that the roof,

once seen as higher than heaven, is merely a
few inches above my head.
That the swing really is nothing more than
chipped white paint over splintered wood;
and the back yard is barren, small, and ragged;
and the closet, is just that, an empty space;
even my father, beautiful and wise as he is, was
really only a man who could not defy his own
fate.

So is there a moment in time when I did not
understand, did not
see the beauty of all that was around me?

That moment is now, and no amount of time
will fix it.
To journey back, would be to ruin the memory
of what was;
to ruin the world as it was meant to be seen-
through eyes of a child.

Tripping Into my World

Shimmering silver,
black winged butterfly;

Shivering gold,
red leaved sky;

Shaking blue,
gray stained water;

Shipping whites,
into bloody slaughter.

Running away,
from yellowed grass;

Roaming free,
upon greening glass;

Raving after,
a pink-fluffed dream;

Ripping apart,
under this blank stream.

Listening to,
the sound of a breeze;

Listing off,
a sniffle and sneeze;

Licking up,
a rainbow lollipop;

Lurking around,
in an empty mountaintop.

Kissing him,
this boy with silver eyes;

Killing her,
the olden who bakes pies;

Kicking them,
those that like to bark;

Keeping it,
the one that leaves it's mark.

Hold yourself hidden,

Run into sight,

Blow out the candle,

Turn on the light;

Don't worry about this,

Keep that in your hand,

Live like we're dying,

Get buried in sand;

Because life is so short,

Step into my life,

Calm your worthless drama,

And ease the damned strife.

Wed. July 17, 2013

She has the potential to project galaxies from
her eyes,
and yet all that can be seen,
is darkened circles,
lonely green,
and a girl who's lost her way.

~ ~

Please, forgive me,
when I cast my eyes downward,
and lose myself in a world unknown to many;
for it is my refuge,
it is my shield,
and I cannot live outside my castle walls.

Turn Around- and You'll Find me Here in the Shadows;

turn around-
and you'll find me here in the shadows;
my way of Thinking seems to upset
you, but not me--

why bother letting me know
when You're the only one Complaining?
keep it to yourself-
there's no one here to listen--

i hate Humanity-
did You Know that your mind Is
superficial, made up of
nothing more than feelings and thought
processes?
crazy, isn't it--

today is Just Another day
living the world we're all confined in-
the Word that left your mouth was
"sexist"--

i laughed at your stupidity-

i thought, For someone as smart
as yourself, you sure give off a lot of idiocy--

and just as you spat your opinion-
i bit back with Animosity.

Who to Blame

If you were to stand upside down in a perfect
line,
Stare out into the horizon,
And watch...

You'd find the world to be a rather odd place.

We stand upright, as it should be,
Or so the law of Gravity says,
And we tend to get blinded by light...

But that's not exactly how it was meant to be,
am I right?

Think of it this way;
The blades of grass beneath your feet were
once emerald green,
And the expanse of sky above your head was
once a blistering blue...

It doesn't look to be that way anymore, does it?

Now you've come to a point in your life in
which you wonder,
Just where did it all go wrong?
The Bible says it was Adam and Eve...

But the scientists say it was the Big Bang.

Of course, we all begin to wonder,
Just who is right?
The politician, the artist?

I say it was no one in particular.

Point your fingers,
Scream your accusations,
And it will get you nowhere...

Unless you were blaming yourself.

As human beings we tend to shy away from
anything that involves hurting ourselves,
At least the sane ones do,
But are the Insane really in the wrong...

Or are we just too scared to admit that we're all
the same?

Picture again that you are standing upside
down in a perfect line,
Staring out into the horizon,
And watching...

What do you see?

A completely different world,
Where everything is truly unstable,
And we're defying the laws of Gravity...

Including yourself.

So who are we to blame,
For the wars,
For the hate,
For the slaughter,
For the rape?

In the end,
When looking at it differently,
We see the one thing that has hidden itself,
So completely, and so utterly, out of sight...

Ourselves.

Within Your Embrace

I want to die within your embrace.
To rip the fabric and shred the lace
that is your fear of awful distaste.

In a world so callous, I will be your
fawn.
A quiet ensemble within a silent yawn,
written by me, your lover at dawn.

The wind blows harshly,
a cold so raw;
but warmth is with me,
the rebel of fall.

So walk down this path
and I'll lead you in tow;
my hand in yours,
to cure your woe.

I'll fight off your monsters,
your fears and disgrace;
if only to lie here and die,
within your embrace.

With all my Soul

My dear,
oh dearest, can you hear me?

Darling, oh love,
what is your calling, or are you simply a dove?

Cooing and crooning,
your quiet song feels sad, yet soothing.

Can I hold your hand,
under a blazing bright sky,
with probing eyes,
and silent sighs?

Stop your song, because it hurts me so;
don't you hear, or don't you know?

I still love you, with all my soul,
and wish to hold you, while we roll and roll;

Down the hill,
under the trees,
past the kids,
and over the seas.

My dearest,
oh dear, can you hear me?

Cooing and crooning,

your quiet song feels sad, yet soothing.

Stop your song, because it hurts me so;
don't you hear, or don't you know?

I still love you, with all my soul,
and hope to hold you,
as we roll and roll;

Through the pastures,
under the caves,
over the hills,
and the rioting raves.

I hope you hear, I hope you know,
that I still love you,
with all my soul.

You and I Need to Dance

Beauty is found best in your eyes-
they spill over with passion and free falling
giggles--
like joy shared in a park on a warm spring
night, where our laughter echoes in the mass of
the moon.

Whisper a message darlin', and I'll listen from
afar-
I can hear your soft voice easily, because we
share a connection--
just like the friction between my tires and the
road as we drive all through the night.

~

Finding your love is somewhat easy, because
there's signs to look out for:
the kindle of warmth in your cheeks when we
speak-
a catch in your voice when your eyes and mine
meet-
the sprinkle of romance that's found in your
speech-
a new kind of air that spreads out and leaks.
~

Bass hugs the night surrounding our bodies-
it fills us up and shakes out our souls as we
shuffle along the dirt--

but I see it in those eyes; you're ready to
go crazy and I'm not about to stop you.

So strap on those fluffies and shed them jeans-
sashay onto the dance floor and pull me there
with you--
cuz you and I need to dance until we collapse
in my car, smoke another cig, and fall in love
with the moon once again.

You Whispered That you Loved Me

I met you at the perfect time.

When my eyes found yours in a crowded
room, I only
Knew that you were handsome, and I
Wished to know your name.

When I went to my car, you asked me if
I was leaving, and you had this look of
Worry in your eyes- I assured you I wasn't.

The relief I saw then made me very happy.

When the fog began to fill the club, I stood on
stage
And began to dance- you seemed surprised
that
I was, in fact, not shy at all.

When I couldn't see anything but clouded
white, your face came into view
And you grabbed my hand, pulled me to the
dance floor, and
We blundered around like children learning to
slow dance for the first time.

The light in your eyes made me feel exactly as
a person should.

When you held me for the first time, it was
merely
Sweet and elegant, something innocent and
Downright adorable.

When your face came close to mine, the
thunderous bass faded away
And our noses barely grazed, the world slowing
Little by little, until your lips, whispering
against mine, finally crashed into me.

Our kisses are like life trickling gently into my
veins.

When you held me last night, your mind
unconscious but
Body moving, you roamed your hands over
every last inch
Of my skin, and your lips left a trail of
crisscrossed flames in my soul.

When our breathing hitched and it seemed
you couldn't surround
Me anymore, your presence would expand
once again, and
My world became enveloped in everything that
is you.

Like a tidal wave, you crashed into me and
swept me into your bottomless depths.

And I was shaking, my core trembling, hands
memorizing
Your shoulders, your jaw, your back, neck, and
arms;
I couldn't believe how anyone could make me
feel so
Beautiful and wanted, even while asleep.

And oh, the way it felt to mold myself to you in
every way-
There is no proper description, no word to
make sense
Of how our souls connected, with marksman
Precision, colliding and fusing as one-

And then you whispered that you loved me.

Woozy

Come on, buttercup, let's cheer up or else just
say Fuck;
Pent up? Write it up, make it loud and shout it
out;
Gimme a few or else I'll spew, choke on words
that fly like birds, in my mouth and out
around, over the town and under those clouds;
Call me Mizz Seusess, the hostess of the
mostest of all the funnest, a girl made famous
with all this lameness;
Or maybe Lady Seussie, old fart Ms. Lucy, a
real messy doozy made oh, so very woozy.

Gloves in the Sky

Twinkled lights, stars so high;
white on blue, black on green;
all the colors in between.

Hands invisible, they seem to fly;
with set coordination and wrist rotations,
seen by so many as an "abomination".

But there is beauty, in this art;
such majesty, glory! All this freedom,
found in a ravers' kingdom.

And this is it, where we start;
born from stars, raised among night;
seizing life and taking flight.

But never do we stray, with hearts so pure,
from where we began, even in horrors we face;
our homeland, our family, our mothers of
space.

Because we are the children of the wonder and
allure;
the tutters, the glovers, the makers of moons!
We children of night, the generation of Lune.

Poi in the Sea

Poignant, perhaps? Maybe genteel, graceful;
yet powerful still.
Like the sea, it ebbs and it flows;
cascading upward and downward,
creating a cycle of cosmic relapse.

Side to side, full-bodied circles;
twisting and turning with the rage of a storm;
never to be broken, never to stop.

Still-framed photos can capture its movements,
but never can they record the full extent,
of the work hidden within.

And so many moons will power it further,
helping it clash into crust and create the land;
the essential flow of life, dedicated entirely to
the strings attached;
hands guiding them together,
hands made from fire,
the people of poi,
the givers of joy.

Dancers on the Ground

Scrap n' stomp,
feet that romp,
eyes ablaze with fire, amaze!

Skin shining,
rhythmic timing,
sweat dripping,
beat hitting;
these are the movements to spark revolutions.

Dust in the air,
kandi to share;
people to meet,
smiles to keep-
songs of souls to beat out our woes.

And here is the build up,
and it's time to gear up,
as the crowd charges on,
hyped for the song,
feet moving faster,
on to a new chapter,
climbing higher and higher,
hoping never to tire,
when suddenly- YES, OH, MY GOD!
The beat drops so hard,
leaving you jarred,
broken and scarred;
stomping, breaking, sliding n' gliding-

dancing with the Earth in a tradition from birth.